ANGRY ANNA

Hey, I'm Crabbie and I love to look out for The Mindful Mermaids. Count how many times you see me throughout the book.

Copyright © 2024
by Lucy Starr
All rights reserved.

No part of this book may be reproduced or used in any manner without written permission of the copyright owner except for the use of quotations in a book review.

For more information: themindfulmermaids@gmail.com

ISBN 978-1-7393728-2-8 (paperback)

www.themindfulmermaids.co.uk

Art makes people happy.
It's something you can't ignore.

But something happened yesterday that really hurt my heart.

I want to be an artist, but I'm super angry. That Scarlett and Serena said those horrible things about me.

I've messed up my studio
by throwing things everywhere.
When I was doing it, I felt better
because I thought I didn't care.

I tried to cheer myself up
by playing with my friends,
but I felt angry when I lost.
I couldn't wait for it to end.

It's impacting my schoolwork.
I think I failed my test.
I wish I knew how to
give my anger a rest.

I've come to a decision.
I want to hurt them too.
I'll make them regret saying those things
if it's the last thing that I do.

So I took her lucky leotard
and threw it in the bin.

Scarlett's in a talent show and she's hoping to come first.

Serena came last in the competition.

Scarlett swam off stage.

I don't know how to explain that I did it out of rage.

I thought I'd feel glad
by making them feel sad.
I should have just been honest
instead of getting mad.

I shouldn't have hurt them because I felt angry

I explained to Serena and Scarlett that I heard them talking about me. I said sorry for what I'd done because I felt angry.

"I'm sorry for what I said"

"I wish I was good at art like you"

"I'm so sorry for what I did"

My friends are fantastic
and they've helped me to see.
I don't need to act out of anger.
There are better ways to be.

I could draw or exercise until I feel happy again.

Of all the things they taught me, there's one I like the best. I'm going to fight feeling angry by taking Starfish Breaths.

Starfish Breaths

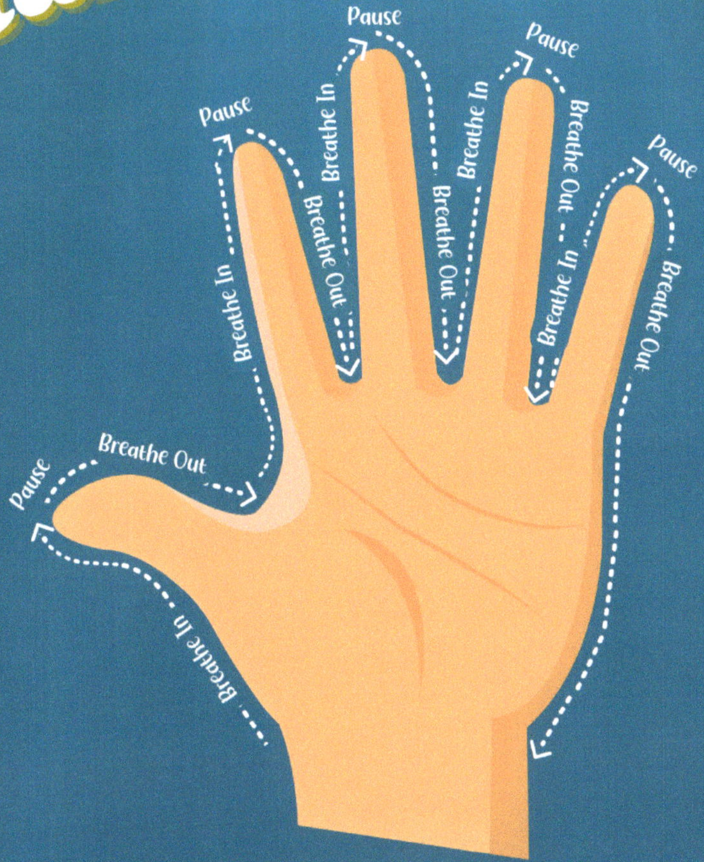

I'll pretend my hand is a starfish
and use my finger to trace all around.
I'll breathe in when I trace up
and breathe out when I trace down.

Sometimes I still feel angry
but I know I'll be okay.
I know how to make myself calm
and make the anger go away.

Discussion Points

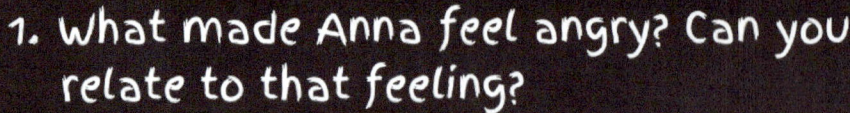

1. What made Anna feel angry? Can you relate to that feeling?
2. How did Anna show that she was angry?
3. Did Anna's anger affect the people around her?
4. Were there any strategies in the book that helped Anna manage her anger?
5. Can you imagine a time when you felt angry like Anna? How did you handle it?
6. Do you think it's okay to feel angry sometimes? Why or why not?
7. Can you think of other emotions that Anna might have felt alongside anger?
8. What did you learn from this book?

These questions are designed to inspire children to engage in critical thinking about the story, its characters, and its underlying themes, all while nurturing their passion for reading and storytelling. They can be tailored to the child's specific age and reading proficiency, ensuring that they are both challenged and encouraged to express their thoughts and ideas.

Check out the Mindful Mermaid Collection

Claim your free gift!

www.ingramcontent.com/pod-product-compliance
Lightning Source LLC
Chambersburg PA
CBHW041522070526
44585CB00002B/45